Goin' Gone

A Fred Koller Songbook

BRIAN KANOF

For Jay,
Best,
Fred Koller
May '96

KATA

Management: Lynn W. Kloss for In Tunes
Piano/Vocal Arrangements by Terry Harr
Music Engraving by Terry Harr
Copy Editor: Cathy Cassinos-Carr
Production Manager: Daniel Rosenbaum
Art Direction: Kerstin Fairbend
Administration: Monica Corton
Director of Music: Mark Phillips
All photos courtesy of Fred Koller.
Cover photography by Señor McGuire:
photo concept and quilt design by KATA

FINALE notation software was used to arrange and
engrave the compositions in this book.

ISBN: 0-89524-674-0

CHERRY LANE MUSIC: THE PRINT COMPANY
EXECUTIVE: Michael Lefferts, President; Kathleen A. Maloney, Director of Customer Service; Rock Stamberg, Advertising and Promotion Manager; Len Handler, Creative Services Manager; Monica Corton, Contracts Administrator; Karen Carey, Division Secretary; Karen DeCrenza, Executive Secretary.
MUSIC: Mark Phillips, Director of Music; Jon Chappell, Associate Director of Music; Gordon Hallberg, Computer Music Engraver; Steve Gorenberg, Music Editor; Kerry O'Brien, Music Editor; Cathy Cassinos-Carr, Copy Editor.
ART: Kerstin A. Fairbend, Art Director; Michele A. Lyons, Assistant Art Director; Rosemary Cappa, Art Assistant.
PRODUCTION: Daniel Rosenbaum, Production Manager; James Piacentino, Production Coordinator.

CONTENTS

KATA

When I bought my first songbook in 1961 at the Melody Mart in downtown Homewood, Ill., I never dreamed that one day I'd be trying to select a dozen-plus songs for my own.

At first, songwriting was a solitary effort for me. But I soon learned to collaborate with other songwriters whose work I admired. (Many of them are represented in this book.) I've written thousands of songs in the past 20 years, and have been greatly blessed to have had a small percentage of them recorded.

Most of the songs in this collection appear on my three albums for Alcazar Records.

—Fred Koller

I would like to especially thank the folks at Cherry Lane, Dolly and Gary at Bug Music, and the indefatigable Lynn Kloss, who have all worked countless hours getting these songs heard.

NOTES ON THE SONGS

by Fred Koller

ANGEL EYES

John Hiatt and I first met in 1974 at the old Exit Inn in Nashville. He was already a staff writer for Tree Music and had just recorded an album with a group called White Duck. We talked about writing together over the years, but never got the opportunity until I brought the Lucrative catalog to Bug Music, which had just opened an office in Nashville. "Angel Eyes" was the first song we wrote together, followed by "Heart to Heart," which Wild Choir recorded. We demoed this song on Steve O'Brien's 8-track and pitched it to a long list of artists, who passed on it. The Jeff Healey cover came after the song was pitched by Dolly Pierce at Bug. It was her first cut as a song plugger. A few weeks later, the song was also recorded by New Grass Revival. There is no feeling that can compare to having a hit on pop radio. I would call Hiatt from across the country as more and more DJ's and listeners responded to the song. The DJ's would make such comments as, "Females are lighting up the phones in Knoxville." I wish I had another hundred songs just like this one.

BOOMTOWN

I wrote this song with Walter Carter for Lacy J. Dalton, one of my oldest friends. Walter and I had each been spending a lot of time outside Nashville in small towns, but it's up to the listener to guess which town this was written about. Unfortunately, it rings true for most of them.

GOIN' GONE

The chorus of this tune is one that Pat Alger had started before we got together. We'd already demoed the song before I ever met "the mysterious" Bill Dale. More than one publisher in Nashville told me that this song was too "folky" for the country market. Nanci Griffith's version led to Kathy Mattea's #1, which has led to numerous covers all around the world. This is sometimes called "The Lighthouse Song."

HEART TO HEART

This song is "the car ride from hell" (we've all had them) set to music. It was first recorded by Gail Davies and Wild Choir, but it needed to be recorded again.

I GOT YOUR NUMBER

I had already written a batch of songs with Al Anderson from N.R.B.Q. when he suggested that he'd like to write with John Hiatt. John was a big Q fan from way back. Big Al had the melody and we had a lyric completed in time to grab some good barbecue from Swett's Dinette for lunch. Albert Lee cut a version that was never released. Dave Edmunds, Big Al, Eddy Raven and yours truly have all had a go at this one. A very "punny" song.

KING AND I

John Gorka is a fine songwriter I first met at the Kerrville Folk Festival. I enjoyed swapping songs with him there and wound up staying at his former residence, the legendary "Blues Palace" in Easton, Pa. All of the tabloids were competing in their coverage of Elvis sightings, so we spent an afternoon looking for the King. This song chronicles what we saw.

LET'S TALK DIRTY IN HAWAIIAN

John Prine will always be one of my favorite songwriters. I was still hanging around Chicago when he and Steve Goodman released their first albums. I'd worn out most of his early records and never grown tired of the wonderful songs he'd written. It was an honor to co-write a song with him. Maybe next time we'll work on one in English. Waka Waka.

LIFE AS WE KNEW IT

Walter Carter and I had already written "Boomtown" for Lacy J. Dalton and were working on separate books about songwriting for Writer's Digest when we wrote this. I'm not sure we even had a title when we started working on the melody. This song had a Louvin Brothers-influenced demo that was sung by Ashley Cleveland and Robb Strandlund.

LITTLE GREEN BUTTONS

Hopefully some of you out there bought this songbook so that you could have the correct words and music to "Goin' Gone" or "Angel Eyes" so that one of these songs could be performed at your wedding. Either song is an excellent choice for such an occasion. This song is not. I've been opening my live shows with this song ever since Shel and I wrote it. Weddings aside, "Little Green Buttons" serves many purposes: 1) It alerts the audience to the fact that I am not your typical "Nashville" singer. 2) It makes them laugh. 3) It makes them think. 4) It makes them realize that every line is important to the song, which makes them listen to the rest of my songs a little bit more closely. Every line in this song is true—except for the lyrics.

KATA

LONE STAR STATE OF MIND

Another first-time collaboration; maybe songwriters try a little harder the first time. Pat Alger and Gene Levine had already had a "folk" hit on "Once in a Very Blue Moon," and Pat had started the chorus to this one before we got together. I didn't meet Gene until long after Nanci Griffith had recorded this song. Pat and I worked on this at his house over by Brown's Diner. Pat had grown up in Georgia and I'd only visited Texas once or twice. I remember early reviews talking about the great song by young Texas writers Koller and Alger … hmm.

SAND IN MY SHOES

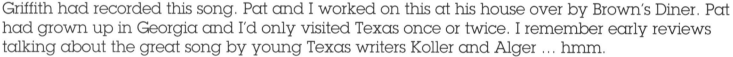

After 15 years of writing songs with other singers in mind, I decided to write something for my own vocal strengths. This was greatly influenced by the work of Harold Arlen, Johnny Mercer, and, believe it or not, Louis Armstrong.

SHE CAME FROM FORT WORTH

"Lone Star State of Mind" revisited. Of course, this time the characters are headed the opposite way. Kathy Mattea's vocal made our little fairy tale seem more real than life. I was down in Texas at the Kerrville Folk Festival when this song went to #1. Went looking for a diner to celebrate in but could only find cafés. I guess nobody else noticed. It's the little details like that that drive me crazy. Pat gave an interview in which he said the waitress was based on a country singer who had moved from Fort Worth to Boulder. I wish he'd mentioned her when we were writing the song.

THIS TOWN

"This Town" is my favorite of the songs that Pat Alger and I have written together. I grew up in a 1950's suburb south of Chicago where the houses and streets were all stamped out of the same cookie cutter used to create communities for the Baby Boomer. I can still remember when the Dutch Elm disease took all of the trees and the neighborhood had that empty, barren look. Like Boomtown, the place

KATA

could be anywhere the listener wanted it to be. What do a boy, a bike and a tree remind you of?

WHEN IT'S GONE

Tom Paxton's songs have been rattling around the back of my head since I was just a teen-age guitarist trying to decide between the Mitchell Trio and the Beatles. Sorry, Tom, the Fab Four won. This song was written for a project organized by One Million Marylanders and McShane Glover, who asked if I had a song I could donate to help raise money and people's consciousnesses through an album of songs that were written about the plight of Chesapeake Bay. It's now out on tape and CD. Buy one for a friend.

Goin' Gone

Moderately slow

Words and Music by
Fred Koller, Pat Alger
and Bill Dale

She Came From Fort Worth

Additional Lyrics

2. And somewhere in the long dark night snow began to fall.
Oh, the world outside was sparkling white when she heard the driver call,
"Everyone off now for Boulder and have a real nice day."
He was waiting on the platform and he raised his hand away.
And she offered no resistance as he took her to his cabin,
And that diner in the distance seemed just like it never happened. *(To Chorus)*

Lone Star State Of Mind

Words and Music by
Fred Koller, Pat Alger
and Gene Levine

Your phone call took me by sur- prise._____ Gee, it's been a long, long time_____

since those hot and hu-mid Tex-as nights we went swim-ming in the tide.

Now, Cor-pus Chris-ti seems so far a-way,
late, late show.

I'm not talk-in' 'bout the miles.
Save the girl and ride a-way.
There's no tell-ing what I'd
I was hop-ing, as those

give to-day
cred-its rolled,
just to see one of your smiles.
he'd make it back to her one day.
Here I sit a-lone in

Den - ver, sip-ping Cal-i-for-nia

in a Lone - star____ state of mind.____

I Got Your Number

Words and Music by
Fred Koller, John Hiatt
and Al Anderson

Moderate Rock

1.Called in-for-ma-tion and I asked them to look,—— 'cause your
2.3. *See additional lyrics*

name was-n't list-ed in the tel-e-phone book. The op-er-a-tor told me it's a

pri-vate line,—— but it starts with a sev-en and it ends with a nine.—— I

Additional Lyrics

2. So I picked up the receiver and I got the dial tone.
I pushed the seven numbers hoping you'd be home.
I couldn't wait to tell you what was on my mind,
But I heard a busy signal at the end of the line.
I waited half a minute and I tried it again.
If you don't hang up, I'm gonna have to bust in. *(To Chorus)*

3. Now there's another busy signal and it's getting late.
What we've got here is a failure to communicate.
I'd do anything just to get you.
Hang it up, baby, and let me through.
It's a real nice invention but at times like this
I can say it so much better with just one more kiss. *(To Chorus)*

Life As We Knew It

Words and Music by
Fred Koller and Walter Carter

pret - ty_____ this time of year._____

This is the end_____ of life as we knew it. You

won't find me liv - ing 'round here._____

Chorus

I loved_____ life as we knew it. I

still can't be-lieve we threw it a-way.

Good-bye, that's all there is to it.

Life as we knew it end-ed to-day.

(Sing 1st time only)

Additional Lyrics

3. I'll leave a number if you need to reach me.
You always called when I had to be gone.
I know here in my memory
Life as we knew it lives on. *(To Chorus)*

Tom Paxton with Fred Koller

Angel Eyes

Words and Music by
Fred Koller and John Hiatt

Slow Rock Ballad

1. Girl,- you're look-ing_____ fine_____ to-night,_____ and ev-'ry guy has__ got you__
2.3. *See additional lyrics*

__ in_____ his__ sight._____ What you're do-in' with a clown_____ like me__

is sure-ly one___ of life's___ lit-tle mys-ter-ies._____ So to-

Additional Lyrics

2. Well, I'm the guy who never learned to dance.
   Never even got one second glance.
   Across the crowded room was close enough.
   I could look but I could never touch. *(To Chorus)*

3. There's just one more thing I need to know:
   If this is love, why does it scare me so?
   It must be something only you can see,
   'Cause, girl, I feel it when you look at me. *(To Chorus)*

When It's Gone

Words and Music by
Fred Koller and Tom Paxton

Additional Lyrics

2. I seen a big sign reading,
   "Don't you come around here."
   It used to be some pretty good water,
   But it died last year.
   Somebody called a meeting,
   Somebody wrote a song,
   Sayin' everybody meant to do something,
   But we waited too long. *(To Chorus)*

3. Oh, the fishermen fish,
   And the sailors sail.
   They been livin' off the water
   Since Jonah and that big ol' whale.
   But we're running out of water
   And we're running out of time.
   You can say that the problem's theirs,
   But it's yours and mine. *(To Chorus)*

Let's Talk Dirty In Hawaiian

Words and Music by
Fred Koller and John Prine

Freely, slowly   **Moderately**

1. Well, I

packed my bags and bought my-self a tick-et____ for the land of the tall palm
2.3.*See additional lyrics*

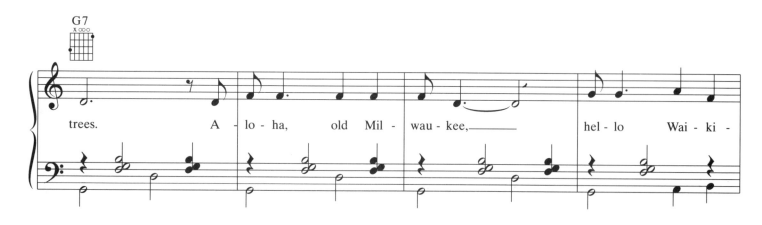

trees.   A-lo-ha, old Mil-wau-kee,____ hel-lo Wai-ki-

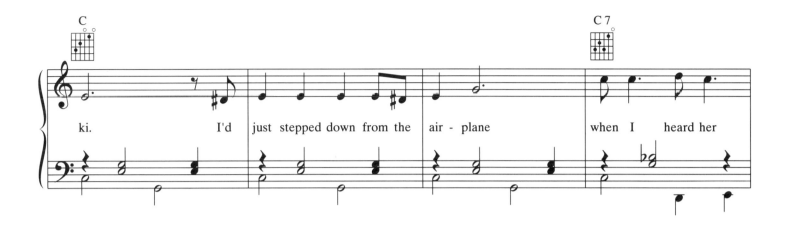

ki. I'd just stepped down from the air - plane when I heard her

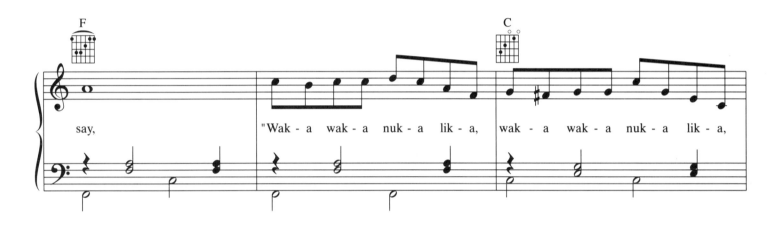

say, "Wak - a wak - a nuk - a lik - a, wak - a wak - a nuk - a lik - a,

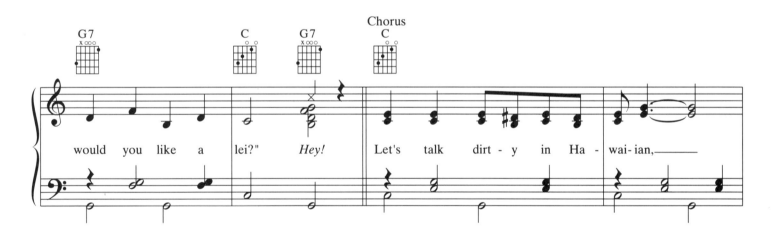

would you like a lei?" *Hey!* Let's talk dirt - y in Ha - wai - ian,_____

Chorus

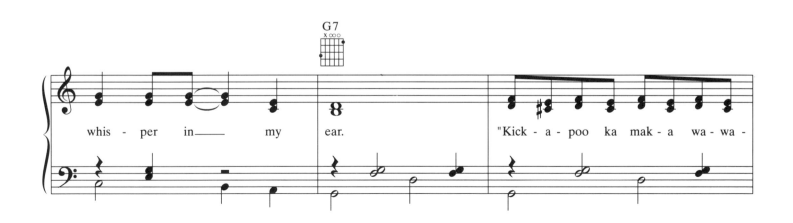

whis - per in____ my ear. "Kick - a - poo ka mak - a wa - wa-

hi - ni" _____ are the words I long to hear.

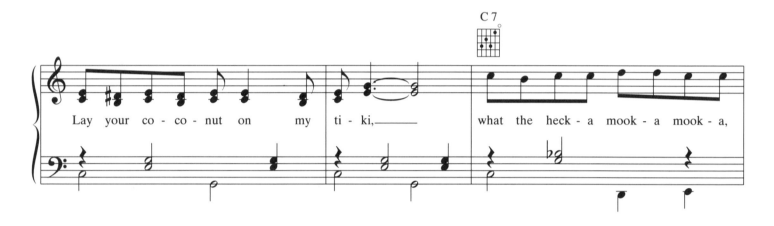

Lay your co - co - nut on my ti - ki, _____ what the heck - a mook - a mook - a,

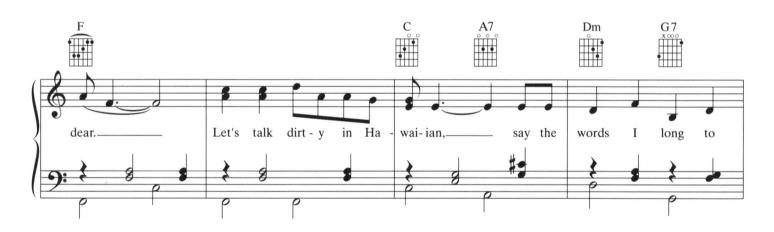

dear. _____ Let's talk dirt - y in Ha - wai - ian, _____ say the words I long to

hear.

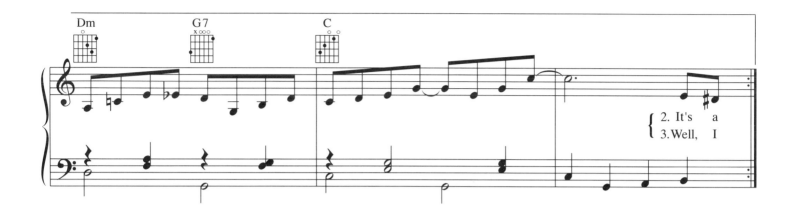

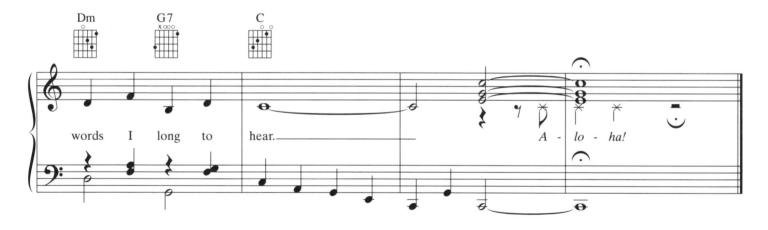

Additional Lyrics

2. It's a ukelele Honolulu sunset.
   Listen to the grass skirts sway.
   Drinking rum from a fresh pineapple
   On Honolulu Bay;
   The steel guitars are playing
   While she's talking with her hands.
   Gimme gimme oka doka,
   Make a wish and wanna polka,
   Words I understand. (*To Chorus*)

3. Well, I bought a lot of junk with my moola
   And I sent it to the folks back home.
   I never had a chance to dance the hula.
   Well, I guess I should have known,
   When you start talkin' to a sweet wahini,
   Walkin' in the pale moonlight;
   Oka doka what a setta knocka
   Rocka sis boom bokas,
   Hope I said it right. (*To Chorus*)

Sand In My Shoes

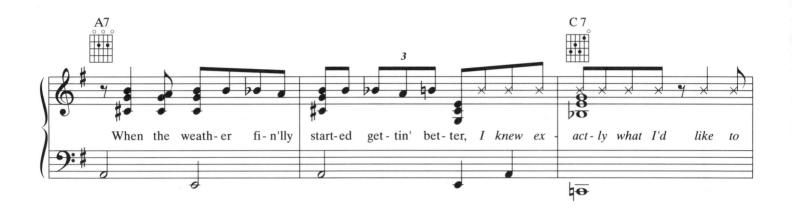

When the weath-er fi-n'lly start-ed get-tin' bet-ter, I knew ex-act-ly what I'd like to

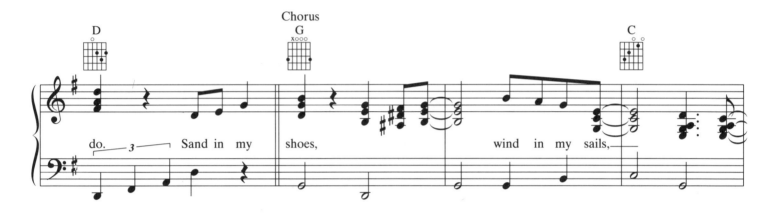

do. Sand in my shoes, wind in my sails,

sun on my back, got the world by the tail.

I wished on a star and it's all com-ing true.

Additional Lyrics

2. Like the motion of a ship on the ocean,
   We keep rockin' along.
   People said we'd never get together.
   I'm so glad they were wrong. *(To Chorus)*

King And I

Words and Music by
Fred Koller and John Gorka

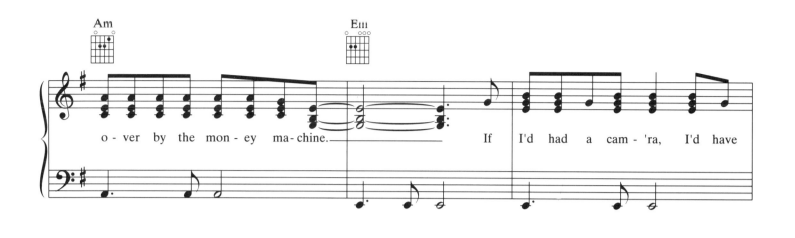

over by the mon - ey ma - chine. _____ If I'd had a cam - 'ra, I'd have

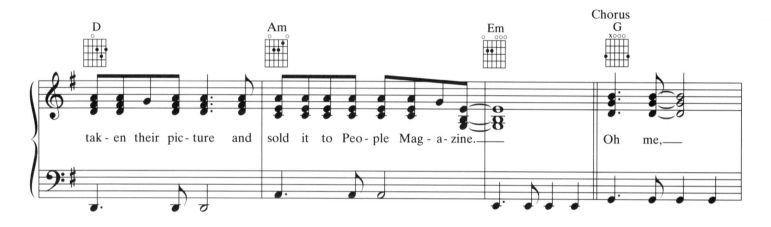

tak - en their pic - ture and sold it to Peo - ple Mag - a - zine. _____ Oh me, _____

oh my, _____ there we were, the King and I. _____ Just a cou - ple of

reg - u - lar guys, _____ hav - ing the time _____ of our lives. _____ 2.3. I saw _____ 4. It was

hav - ing the time___ of our lives.___ We were

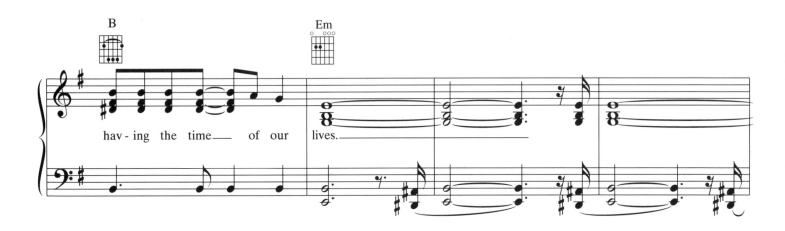

hav - ing the time___ of our lives.___

Additional Lyrics

2. I saw Elvis Presley and John Belushi
   Hitchhicking down the avenue.
   When I picked them up and asked who they were,
   They both said, "Howard Hughes."
   And I know it was him at the laundromat,
   Trying to change a five,
   'Cause he carried some jumpsuits to a White Cadillac
   That was parked on the curb outside. *(To Chorus)*

3. I saw Elvis at the Strike and Spare,
   Bowling a three hundred game.
   He'd put on some weight and he'd lost some hair,
   But he was still the King, just the same.
   Later that night, I followed him home
   To a trailer at the end of the road.
   Elvis got some beers and we sat outside
   And we waited for the U.F.O.'s. *(To Chorus)*

4. It was Elvis Presley and Yul Brenner,
   And Yul said he belonged in this song.
   But Elvis said, "Yul, go shave your head,
   It's already way too long." *(To Chorus)*

Little Green Buttons

Words and Music by
Fred Koller and Shel Silverstein

Additional Lyrics

3. Now she's living in a house of love.
   She's got his attention and he can't get enough.
   He spends every evening trying to undo
   The little green buttons
   On her birthday suit. *(To Chorus)*

Boomtown

Words and Music by
Fred Koller and Walter Carter

Additional Lyrics

2. Now, Farmer Johnson's cornfield
   Is sproutin' little houses.
   The dozer got the scarecrow,
   They hauled his cows away.
   Down around the courthouse,
   Oh, you can smell the money.
   Like bees after honey,
   They're here to stay. *(To Chorus)*

3. There's pictures in the paper
   From all around the country
   Of chrome-plated shovels
   Breakin' new ground.
   When the wheels of progress
   Roll like thunder,
   It kind of makes you wonder
   If they'll ever slow down. *(To Chorus)*

Heart To Heart

Words and Music by
Fred Koller and John Hiatt

Additional Lyrics

2. You know we never did nothin' before
We couldn't talk about.
If I'd known this was the road to nowhere
I might have took a different route.
Side by side, starin' straight ahead,
Have you heard a single word I said?
The road is gettin' rough,
I believe I've had enough
Of feeling like I've been misled. *(To Chorus)*

This Town

Words and Music by
Fred Koller and Pat Alger

1.This is the way I re-mem-
2. *See additional lyrics*

ber this town, sleep-y and qui-et and warm. A fine, green mist is

all that re-mains from a late af-ter-noon thun-der-storm. Soon, the

street-lights will shine on the side-walk where a kid left his bike in the rain.

And in the twi-light sky___ I can squint up my eyes and this old town still looks the

Chorus

same. I came to this town___ to re-mem - ber___

mf

some - bod - y I___ used to be, a kid who be - lieved___ he could see___

___ the whole world___ from the top of a mul - ber - ry tree.

Additional Lyrics

2. I'll circle the block, and I'll park 'cross the street
From the house where each Saturday night
I talked about places that I'd never been,
Till your father flashed the hall light.
And sometimes it feels like a long time ago,
And sometimes it's just like yesterday.
It doesn't take long in this sleepy old town
For me to believe I could stay. *(To Chorus)*

KATA

Available on Alcazar Records
(Box 429, Waterbury, VT 05676)
The Night Of The Living Fred
Songs From The Night Before
Where The Fast Lane Ends

Available from Writer's Digest Books
(1507 Dana Ave., Cincinnati, OH 45207)
How To Pitch and Promote Your Songs

Fred is also available for songwriting workshops.
Contact: Lynn W. Kloss
In Tunes
519 Tilden Avenue
Teaneck, NJ 07666
(201) 836-1315